JEFFERSON'S DREAM

ALSO BY JOHN PERRAULT

*THE BALLAD OF LOUIS WAGNER AND OTHER
NEW ENGLAND STORIES IN VERSE*

HERE COMES THE OLD MAN NOW

Jefferson's Dream

The Ballad of the Declaration of Independence

With Accompanying CD of
Original Ballads
Profiling Eight Great Americans
Who Ploughed Jefferson's Field

John Perrault

HOBBLEBUSH BOOKS
Brookline, New Hampshire

Composed in Warnock Pro at Hobblebush Books

Printed in the United States of America

Photo of author by John W. Hession,
courtesy of the photographer

Piano transcriptions by Barbara London

Publisher's Cataloging-In-Publication Data
(Prepared by The Donohue Group, Inc.)

Perrault, John.
  Jefferson's dream : the ballad of the Declaration of Independence / John Perrault.

    p. : ill., music ; cm. + 1 CD

  "With accompanying CD of original ballads profiling eight great Americans who ploughed Jefferson's field."
  CD contains original music by John Perrault. Book contains sheet music and lyrics printed as text to the songs on the CD.
  Includes bibliographical references.
  ISBN: 978-0-9801672-7-6

1. United States. Declaration of Independence—In literature. 2. Statesmen—United States—Biography—Poetry. 3. Statesmen—United States—Biography. 4. Statesmen—United States—Songs and music. 5. Ballads, English—United States. I. Title.

E176 .P47 2009

920.073   2009931191

Published by:

HOBBLEBUSH BOOKS
17-A Old Milford Road
Brookline, New Hampshire 03033

www.hobblebush.com

For Art Meyer

. . . And say, finally, whether peace is best preserved
by giving energy to the government or information to
the people. This last is the most certain and the most
legitimate engine of government. Educate and inform
the whole mass of the people. Enable them to see that
it is their interest to preserve peace and order, and they
will preserve them. And it requires no very high degree
of education to convince them of this. They are the only
sure reliance for the preservation of our liberty.

—THOMAS JEFFERSON

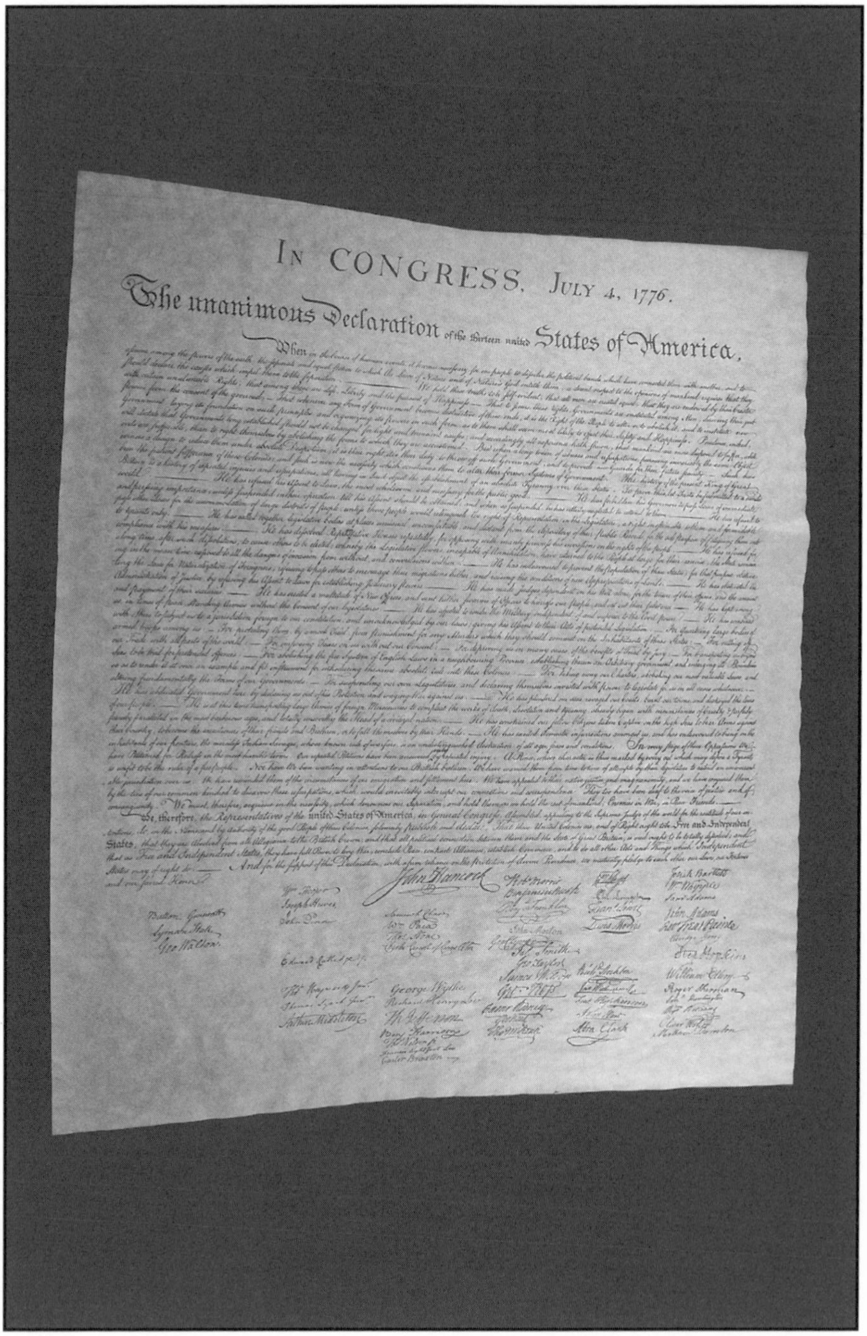
IN CONGRESS, JULY 4, 1776.
The unanimous Declaration of the thirteen united States of America,

How To Use This Book

Dear Teachers & Readers,

A S YOU WEIGH THIS BOOK OF BALLADS in your hands, please trust the scale to read on the light side—on the singing side of things. Light as in wakening to ideas—singing as in saying them out.

The question arises—start with the text or with the songs? This is akin to asking the author which comes first, the words or the music? There is no one answer. The most accurate might be that they sort of happen together.

There is no right way to engage *Jefferson's Dream*. One teacher tells us listening to a particular ballad first sets just the tone for taking up text and related materials. Another says a ballad connects best after working with the larger lesson plan. Both may say that encouraging students to sing the songs—and better yet, make up some verses of their own—makes for full engagement with these eight great Americans.

Some students may not be ready to digest the text on their own—their teachers may choose to summarize these pages in hand-outs. Other students may relish the challenge of reading the text and even trying their hand at writing new ballads on other historical figures.

Clearly, there is no right order of presentation. A unit on slavery, for example, might include the ballads on Tubman, Lincoln, Douglass, and Thoreau without involving the others. And the core values of the Declaration of Independence might be successfully approached by working backward from Eleanor Roosevelt, to Douglass, to Lincoln, and finally, to Jefferson.

One thing is fundamental, however. The lives of the eight figures here—along with their ideas—come into felt focus only by merging text with song. Each song is a ballad—a short narrative poem meant to be sung. But the whole book is a ballad in a larger sense: it strives to make the story of the Declaration of Independence sing in our hearts.

Contents

Preface

My high school history teacher grimaced in pain whenever he heard a student confuse the Declaration of Independence with the United States Constitution. He'd probably suffer cardiac arrest hearing adults make the same error today. To my mind, this is no small matter. The reports are out there: millions of Americans don't know much about history—especially their own. If we are unaware of the core documents that forged our very liberties, what does that say about our notion of patriotism?

Pledging allegiance to the flag does not alone make a patriot. It begs the question: what does the flag represent? Reflection suggests it is the visual expression of our ideals, values, history and law. And that points us to the Declaration of Independence and the Constitution. If we don't know anything about either, how can we honestly say we love our country? We might as well pledge allegiance to ignorance.

This book is both an effort to recall and salute the lives of eight Americans who represent the core values of the Declaration and an argument: freedom comes with a price tag—we have to pay for it by study and exercise. We can only know what it really means by rediscovering its roots and watering its soil. If the noble ideas articulated in the Declaration of Independence are to continue to have any effect, then, as Eleanor Roosevelt argued for the Universal Declaration of Human Rights, the people must know them, understand them, and demand adherence to them. That demand applies to government as well as to the people themselves.

The Declaration says we all have basic rights and we're all created equal. True or false? Think about it—if it's not true—what Jefferson wrote back in 1776—then who are we as a people? What do we stand for as a nation? How can we claim justice as our cause? But—if it is true—then doesn't it seem we still have a long way to go? This book—these ballads—are an attempt to revisit this fundamental question.

I am grateful to my publisher, Sid Hall of Hobblebush Books, for his insight and acumen in producing the book, and Hobblebush Marketing Director Amy Wood for her creative assistance; to Holly Perrault for closely reading and editing the text; to Barbara London for her expert musical transcriptions of the songs; and to my dear musician friends Mike Rogers, Jim MacDougall, Ellie May Shufro, Barbara London, Rick Kress, Susie Burke, David Surrette and Rick Watson who helped me survive the recording process intact. I am grateful to Eve Corey, Mary Jane Rowan, and Lisa Graziano for floating my ballads on the waters of their classrooms, and to Maryhop Brandon for her support and encouragement. Thanks are also in order to my ever patient, ever talented engineer, Jeff Landrock, who mixed and mastered, and to Barbara, Mike, Rick, Tracie and Kristen, who lent their ears to the process. Finally, my thanks to Tom Daly of Crooked Cove Records for the CD production, John W. Hession for his photograph, and Art Meyer for sharing his love of history and passion for justice.

Introduction

The Declaration of Independence, July 4, 1776: *... We hold these truths to be self evident, that all men are created equal, that they are endowed by their Creator with certain unalienable Rights, that among these are Life, Liberty and the pursuit of Happiness.*

These are the words of Thomas Jefferson, confirmed by the drafting committee he led, and adopted by the Continental Congress. These words evoke the vision our Founders had of what America means, a vision that puts the individual (because sacrosanct) before the state:

... That to secure these rights, Governments are instituted among Men, deriving their just powers from the consent of the governed,—That whenever any form of Government becomes destructive of these ends it is the right of the People to alter or to abolish it, and to institute new Government, laying its foundation on such principles and organizing its powers in such form as to them shall seem most likely to effect their Safety and Happiness.

Idealism? Or existential reality? Abraham Lincoln answered this question by equating the Declaration's concepts of equality and liberty with rights that could only be more gradually realized over time. To him, this is what the drafters meant:

> They meant simply to declare the *right*, so that the *enforcement* of it might follow as fast as circumstances should permit. They meant to set up a standard maxim for free society, which should be familiar to all, and revered by all; constantly looked to, constantly labored for, and even though never perfectly attained, constantly approximated, and thereby constantly spreading and deepening its influence, and augmenting the happiness and value of life to all people of all colors everywhere.

Jefferson's vision has been ridiculed as a dream at various times in our history. Too often that ridicule has flowed from minds seduced by the gospel of greed. Is it really true that the hearts of women and men are moved only by money? Certainly Lincoln did not accept this. He abhorred the notion that the only true principle of right action was self-interest. Lincoln believed in the transcending human values expressed in the Declaration as true and abiding for all people everywhere. If those principles were not always realized in fact, the Declaration provided the beacon to follow in the constant human struggle for justice.

So when Martin Luther King rings out "I Have a Dream" at the Lincoln Memorial in 1963, he means what Lincoln meant—a dream in this sense: the sacred goal. Liberty and equality for all races, all genders, all faiths, all peoples. Lincoln had made it explicit. There was "something in that Declaration giving liberty, not alone to the people of this country, but hope to the world for all future time."

How many nations—peoples—movements—, have acted out of fidelity to this "Dream." How many hearts have been lifted to carry on in sight of this "Dream." How many years—decades—centuries now, and the "Dream" still not fully in focus—not quite there as we gradually, progressively, wake to the reality of its meaning.

In this book and these ballads I focus on eight historical figures who took the Declaration to heart—either explicitly, by publicly advocating its values, or implicitly, by living them. Besides Jefferson and Lincoln, here are Harriet Tubman, Frederick Douglass, Elizabeth Cady Stanton, Henry David Thoreau, Ida B. Wells and Eleanor Roosevelt. They don't all agree with one another in the practical world of political action, but their visions tend to cohere when it comes to racial equality and liberty. And it is the women who get the men to see that advancing the cause of racial equality ultimately demands advocating for gender equality and women's suffrage.

Don't expect to find saints here. Just real men and women who looked fear in the face and persevered. Just eight strong Americans who carried the Declaration of Independence in the open book of their hearts.

JEFFERSON'S DREAM

Thomas Jefferson

THOMAS JEFFERSON

Born—   April 13, 1743, Albemarle County, Virginia

Youth—   Home-tutored, College of William and Mary, reader, horseman, fiddler, dancer

Maturity— Law, politics, family, Monticello, American Philosophical Society, Secretary of State, President; Significant Writings: Declaration of Independence (1776), *Notes on the State of Virginia* (1785), Statute of Virginia for Religious Freedom (1786), First Inaugural Address (1801)

Words—   "The abolition of domestic slavery is the great object of desire in those colonies where it was unhappily introduced in their infant state. But previous to the enfranchisement of the slaves we have, it is necessary to exclude all further importations from Africa . . . "

                    —*A Summary View of the Rights of British America (1774)*

Died—   July 4, 1826, Charlottesville, Virginia

"Jefferson's Dream"

What makes a nation? How does one begin? How does it keep going? For clarification: nations are not governments. Political regimes come and go, while nations stand steady. A nation means a people—a people who speak the same language, follow the same customs, share the same values, hold sacred the same symbols, love the same land. But how does "a people" come to be? In Europe and Asia we might be looking to myth and legend for the answer. In the United States, we can watch a nation unfold on paper.

America's founding—its grounding—is historically present for all to see. It is stated and explained in the Declaration of Independence. Never before in history had a nation been specifically founded on its main philosophical premise: the individual before the state. Natural rights before political rights. Political legitimacy dependent on the consent of the governed. The people as sovereign. The Declaration of Independence is our rational myth—our public religion. Equality and Liberty for all. With these two claims in hand, Americans set forth to forge their destiny. It has proved a constant struggle. Every generation has come up against the tension inherent in the merging of these two standards. It is proving to be an ongoing process, an ongoing experiment. And it is far from over.

The ideas articulated in the Declaration don't appear out of thin air. There are Magna Carta, the English Bill of Rights, the various founding charters of the thirteen colonies, and a whole crop of European philosophical writings that stand behind their evolution. Jefferson himself said he was only expressing the common sense of the matter when writing the preamble. Yet it is Jefferson's felicitous words that capture the essence of the political mind of the times and that have stood the test of time. It is these words that have inspired millions over the centuries to risk their lives for the ideas they so eloquently express.

How is it that Jefferson came to be the one to articulate the founding values of the American experiment? His personal history is a far cry from the more radical and risk-taking stories of Thomas Paine and Patrick Henry. Jefferson grew up with books in comfortable surroundings, tended by slaves. As a young man he took to horses, the fiddle, the ladies and the dance. But while at William and Mary he came under the tutelage of serious philosophical thinkers—most notably William Small and George Wythe. Through Small, Jefferson was grounded in the culture of the Scottish Enlightenment; through Wythe, Jefferson learned his law. Arguably, Jefferson's commitment to the moral imperative of democratic principles was fundamentally intellectual in nature.

Let us confront the hypocrisy question right up front. Jefferson was a slaveholder. Over two hundred slaves: building, preserving, serving, feeding, supporting the grand home he called "Monticello." Recent evidence suggests that after his wife's death, he had an intimate relationship with Sally Hemmings, a black servant to his daughter Mary, and that he fathered children by her. At the time of his death, except for a certain few, Jefferson failed to free his slaves under his will.

Yet it remains historical fact that in the Declaration Jefferson included a long passage, struck out by the Congress, condemning the slave trade on moral grounds. He also introduced a provision in a plan of legislative reform for Virginia that would have declared free all slaves born after a certain date. And in his *Notes on Virginia*, he wrote:

> The whole commerce between master and slave is a perpetual exercise of the most boisterous passions, the most unremitting despotism on the one part and degrading submissions on the other . . . I tremble for my country when I reflect that God is just . . .

The essence of hypocrisy is preaching one thing and doing another—the opposite in fact. All kinds of excuses may be raised by all kinds of "Jeffersonians" for all kinds of reasons—but, try as they might, they can't erase history. So the answer is: "Yes, there is hypocrisy there." But does this by definition end the matter?

Does the fact that Jefferson was a slave owner in any way make the Declaration of Independence false? That Jefferson held slavery to be a vicious assault on human dignity and freedom is a matter of record. That he condemned slavery as immoral and a threat to the very foundation of the Republic may fly in the face of his personal behavior, but that behavior in no way refutes the rightness of that condemnation.

Jefferson said "*All men* are created equal" and left the women out. Perhaps it goes without saying that including women never entered his mind—or the mind of any of the founders for that matter. (Perhaps excepting John Adams, whose wife Abigail constantly reminded him to not forget the women.) The critical thing here is that the language Jefferson used allowed for the evolution of his terms, making possible the inclusion of every human being, black or white, man or woman, as Lincoln argued some eighty-two years later.

It is the great Frederick Douglass who tags Jefferson "the sage of the Old Dominion," and who reminds us Jefferson knew "one hour" of a slave's bondage was "worse than ages of the oppression your fathers (the American Revolutionaries) rose in rebellion to oppose." When you read Jefferson on the subject of slavery you come away with the picture of a man who deplored the subjugation of the Black Race, yet lacked the necessary will to back his words with bold political action. If we can fault him on the latter, it is necessary to hail him for the former—his words—which, coming into the mouths of a Douglass and a Lincoln, prove the historic voice and enactment of the most fundamental political and cultural change this nation has ever experienced. Jefferson lived a life of inconsistencies, but the words he uttered in the Declaration of Independence—words so eloquently invoked by Dr. King at the Lincoln Memorial in 1963—continue to ring like a fire bell in the night.

What, then, are we to make of this Jefferson? This complex and seemingly contradictory man? In my ballad, I suggest that his "Dream" allows him to see that his words will be taken up by future generations in a larger and perhaps more creative sense than eighteenth century political pragmatism would allow. In his "Dream" he imagines the use to which Lincoln will put his prophetic lines.

If this be too radical an implication of a mystical element in a fundamentally rational political life, it perhaps doesn't go as far as the facts surrounding Jefferson's death—July 4, 1826—occurring fifty years to the date of the signing of the Declaration of Independence, and just an hour or two before the passing of his dear friend and political rival, John Adams. We know what John Quincy Adams read (by Proclamation) into the circumstances of the passing of Jefferson and Adams:

> In this most singular coincidence, the finger of Providence is plainly visible! It hallows the Declaration of Independence as the Word of God, and is the bow in the Heavens that promises its principles shall be eternal, and their dissemination universal over the Earth.

We are free to make of it as we will; but the timing of the events is an incontrovertible fact.

Words and Music
© 2009 by John Perrault

Jefferson's Dream

Jefferson's Dream

Lyrics

My name is Thomas Jefferson, I wrote the Declaration
And I set the stage to free the slaves although I owned two hundred of them;
when I wrote that Document "We hold these truths self-evident,
all men are equal" what I meant was all humanity.

Chorus:
Freedom, Reason, everything in season,
Liberty, Equality, patience friend, this won't be easy;
Reason, Freedom, that's what I believe in,
America of Thee I sing.

I served General Washington, I had to battle Hamilton,
I wrote my *Notes* with every hope we'd work the land and love the land;
all Federalists, Republicans, John Adams and James Madison,
I came to embrace both of them, they came to embrace me.

Chorus:
Freedom, Reason, everything in season, Liberty, Equality, educating everybody . . . etc.

"A fire bell, a fire storm," you can't enslave a man for long,
"I trembled for my nation's laws, when God is just" and we are wrong;
I passed the torch to Abraham to use my Declaration
and save the Union, save the Nation, ending slavery.

Chorus:
Freedom, Reason, everything in season, Liberty, Equality, "Nature's Aristocracy" . . . etc.

I lived in France, I looked to Rome, Virginia was always home,
I built my house down in the South, my mountain villa Monticello;
all my family, my dear children, Martha, Sally, all you pilgrims,
welcome, Thomas Jefferson, says welcome to my door.

Chorus:
Freedom, Reason, everything in season, Liberty, Equality, "Toleration," that's my
    creed . . . etc.

Harriet Tubman

Harriet Tubman (1823–1913)
nurse, spy and scout

HARRIET TUBMAN

Born— Circa 1820, Dorchester County, Maryland

Youth— Brodess Estate, Miss Susan's household, religious inculcation, head injury from Barrett Overseer, Stewart Lumber work

Maturity— Marriage to John Tubman, escape, Underground Railroad, John Brown connection, Civil War experience, Charity House, Auburn, NY; Speeches: July 4, 1859 speech at Framingham; Speech to Special Session on Women's Suffrage at New England Anti-Slavery Society Conference, Boston, 1860; Speech on Dedication of Tubman Home for Charity, June 23, 1908

Words— "I did not take up this work for my own benefit, but for those of my race who need help. The work is now well started and I know God will raise up others to take care of the future."
                              —Dedication of Tubman Home for Charity

Died— March 10, 1913, Auburn, New York

"Ballad of Harriet Tubman"

Harriet Tubman was born Arimenta Ross in Dorchester County, Maryland, three years after Frederick Douglass was born. One of eleven children, and born into slavery, she was hired out by her parents at the age of five to work as a nursemaid for a comfortable white couple. By the age of twelve she was working in the fields. By her early teens she knew well the burn of the lash and the brutality of the system that ruled her. Blocking an overseer from whipping a young black slave for some perceived infraction, her head was smashed by a two-pound weight hurled by the overseer at the fleeing man. Rendered unconscious for several days, Harriet never completely recovered from the blow and suffered blackouts all her life.

Harriet was not literate. How amazing then to realize this woman would become one of the most heroic exponents of the ideals expressed in the Declaration. How can that be? Harriet never read the document. She never had the opportunity to learn to read, let alone be schooled in the ideas of the Enlightenment. Yet she seems to have carried in her heart a basic understanding of and appreciation for the sanctity of the individual. Perhaps the answer lies in the Declaration itself—the assertion that equality and liberty are qualities inherent to the human condition. We know this, says Jefferson, because it is self-evident. We know this—now more clearly—because Abraham Lincoln and Martin Luther King have explained to us just what those self-evident truths really mean. Harriet probably knew it better than most because her life was fundamentally violated by slave masters who refused to believe it. Either they were in denial of the Declaration's preamble or in denial of Harriet's humanity.

Whatever their position, Harriet's position was clear: wrong on both counts. She manifested her natural grasp of human dignity and fundamental rights by standing up to the masters' indefensible ideology. And she clearly had no lack of courage. At the age of twenty-five she married John Tubman, a free black man, and constantly, quietly, raged at her slave status. After learning that she and family members would probably soon be sold south, she began planning her escape. Unable to convince John to accompany her on the journey north, she gathered up her two brothers and struck out for freedom. Although her brothers finally turned back, Harriet made it to Philadelphia with the help of certain "conductors" on the underground railroad. Thereafter, she devoted her life to helping other slaves—more than three hundred of them—work their way north to freedom, becoming the legendary "Moses to her people."

Tubman became involved in the abolitionist campaigns. She knew Douglass and was encouraged by the passion of his voice. Douglass, in turn, celebrated her as a fearless champion of an enslaved people. John Brown considered her worthy of sainthood. Had it not been for illness, she would have joined Brown at his infamous raid at Harper's Ferry. During the Civil War she became a spy for the Union in South Carolina and led a small force behind enemy lines up the Combahee River to successfully rouse over six hundred slaves to flee the plantations and relocate under the protection of Federal forces.

Harriet railed at Lincoln's failure to immediately emancipate the slaves at the start of the war, and never had much sympathy for the political explanations that stood back of that failure. She would not brook compromise when it came to the question of slavery and was constantly risking her own life to remedy that great evil. Nonetheless, she was embraced by Lincoln's secretary of state, William Seward, who advocated her cause and arranged for her to finally acquire a home of her own in his home town of Auburn, New York.

Harriet was not an orator like Douglass. We have no record of her specifically calling upon the principles of the Declaration of Independence to ground her calling for emancipation of the slaves. But her natural born commitment to the ideals expressed in Jefferson's document and her dramatic forays into a hostile South with a price on her head to lead slaves to freedom speak volumes about the resonance of Jefferson's words. She proves one of the most credible witnesses to Lincoln's conviction that something far deeper than self-interest motivates the human soul to act rightly.

In her later days, Harriet's association with Elizabeth Cady Stanton's Suffrage Movement and her charitable work on behalf of the disadvantaged demonstrate her profound understanding of what justice really means. In her heart she knew the Declaration's affirmation of liberty and equality for all, even if she never was able to read the text.

In 1990, in declaring March 10 a day to honor Harriet Tubman, then President George H. Bush stated the proposition unequivocally:

> In celebrating Harriet Tubman's life, we remember her commitment to
> freedom and rededicate ourselves to the timeless principles she struggled

to uphold. Her story is one of extraordinary courage and effectiveness in the movement to abolish slavery and to advance the noble ideals enshrined in our Nation's Declaration of Independence: "We hold these truths to be self-evident, that all men are created equal, that they are endowed by their Creator with certain unalienable Rights, that among these are Life, Liberty and the pursuit of Happiness."

Words and Music
© 2009 by John Perrault

Ballad of Harriet Tubman

She was the

Verses:

Mo-ses to her peo-ple   Ar-i-men-ta was her name—   She had a

boun-ty on her head—   for steal-ing slaves—.

Slipped on-to plan-ta-tions where she   up and cut their chains—   Let

Har-ri-et   lie eas-y   in her grave.   Let

Chorus:

Har-ri-et rest eas-y   in the marsh-es,   Let

Har-ri-et   rest eas-y in   the clay.   To-

day if she came back a-gain   and looked out on the prom—ise land, oh I

won-der   just what Har-ri-et   would say.

Ballad of Harriet Tubman (continued)

Bridge:

Twelve years old she took the blow that drove in-to her brain—

Slav-er flung a hunk— of rock her— way,

Suf-fered black-outs all her life, oh they hit her like a train, Let

Har-ri-et lie eas-y in her— grave.

Ballad of Harriet Tubman

Lyrics

She was the Moses to her people
Arimenta was her name
Had a bounty on her head for stealing slaves—

Slipped onto plantations
Where she up and cut their chains—
Let Harriet lie easy in her grave.

Chorus:
Let Harriet rest easy in the marshes
Let Harriet rest easy in the clay—
Today if she came back again
And looked out on the Promised Land
I wonder just what Harriet would say.

Born in 1820
On the shores of Maryland,
Farmed out to work at ten years old a slave—

Whippings came as regular
As blisters to her hands—
Let Harriet lie easy in her grave.

Bridge:
Twelve years old she took the blow
That drove into her brain—
Slaver flung a hunk of rock her way
Suffered black-outs all her life,
Hit her like a train—
Let Harriet lie easy in her grave.

North to Philadelphia
With nothing but her faith—
Nothing but her legs to navigate—

Joined the secret railroad
Underground and unafraid—
Let Harriet lie easy in her grave.

Chorus: Let Harriet rest easy in the meadows . . .

Three hundred souls conducted
On the rails to liberty—
To Canada she guided all the way—

Every time she went back south
She risked the gallows tree—
Let Harriet lie easy in her grave.

Bridge:
She scouted out the rebels
For the Federals in the South—
Made contact with the blacks for their escape—
Deep in Carolina
She got six hundred of them out—
Let Harriet lie easy in her grave.

New York State at Auburn
There's a house that burns a light—
There's a face in a photo looking grave—

She lived the Declaration,
You can see it in her eyes—
Let Harriet lie easy in her grave.

Chorus: Let Harriet rest easy in the mountains . . .

Abraham Lincoln

ABRAHAM LINCOLN

Born—   February 12, 1809, Sinking Spring Farm, Hardin County, Kentucky

Youth—   Backwoods, books, river rafter, rail splitter, storyteller

Maturity—   Shopkeeper, postmaster, politics, law, congressman, President; Significant Writings: Address to Young Men's Lyceum of Springfield (1838); Speech at Springfield (1857); Speech in Philadelphia (1861); First Inaugural Address (1861); Gettysburg Address (1863); Second Inaugural Address (1865)

Words—   "This *declared* indifference (to the spread of slavery) . . . I cannot but hate. I hate it because of the monstrous injustice of slavery itself. I hate it because it deprives our republican example of its just influence in the world—enables the enemies of free institutions, with plausibility, to taunt us as hypocrites—causes the real friends of freedom to doubt our sincerity, and especially because it forces so many really good men amongst ourselves into an open war with the very fundamental principles of civil liberty—criticizing the Declaration of Independence, and insisting that there is no right principle of action but *self-interest.*"

—Speech at Peoria, 1854

Died—   April 15, 1865, Washington, D.C.

"Abe Lincoln Walks at Midnight"

To the record of our greatest president, what can we possibly add? That he was sad is a given. But such a sadness it was—born, perhaps, in the early grief at his mother's loss. Honed by the harsh reality of life on the frontier. Exacerbated by the death of two beloved sons. Matured by the tragic wisdom gained as he faced the burden of saving a people bent on self-destruction.

That he preserved the Union is also a given. But at such a price. Every aching bone in his body was dedicated to that effort from the moment he stepped forward to strive for political office. And he took that aching for the sacrifice he was meant to make, even as Lee laid down his arms at Appomattox—even as Booth prepared his hour upon the stage.

Lincoln understood that a nation sown on the grounds of liberty and equality must constantly tend to its growing. The United States possessed no Homer or Moses. Our gods were words, prophesied in the Declaration of Independence and made flesh in the Constitution. Those words, dispersed on the winds of the Revolution, required cultivation, irrigation, interpretation. The American experiment could only possibly succeed if the people went out to the fields and worked with their noble crop of words. Every season could bring a new understanding of what it means to be free. People must be free to enjoy the fruits of their hard labor, yes, but full human freedom must not be confused with mere getting and spending. Freedom for Lincoln was essentially political in nature—a condition made possible by a just state for the sake of the public good. And he understood that "good" to be far different and greater in value than any millionaire's bank account.

Dred Scott was a slave from Missouri. His master took him to Illinois where he lived for eleven years. Illinois was a free state. He also went to the free territory of Wisconsin. Subsequently he was taken back to Missouri. He sued for his freedom, arguing his time in Illinois made him a free man. The case went from the state court in Missouri up to the United States Supreme

Court. There, Chief Justice Taney wrote the infamous opinion that held Scott had no standing to sue because he was not a citizen of the United States under the Constitution. He was a slave. And slaves were not citizens.

Quoting the Declaration of Independence, Taney maintained that "the enslaved African race were not intended to be included, and formed no part of the people who framed and adopted this declaration . . . The unhappy black race were separated from the white by indelible marks, and laws long before established, and were never thought of or spoken of except as property . . . "

Taney's statements on the Declaration set no legal precedent, however; and Justice Curtis' majestic dissent makes a strong case that Taney's interpretation is historically unfounded, inconsistent with the legal record, and logically wrong.

In countering the position taken by Justice Taney, Lincoln argued that just because the Declaration did not actually place blacks on an equal footing with whites, this did not mean that the intent was to exclude them. The Declaration did not put all whites on an equal footing either. In a speech given at Springfield, Illinois in 1857, Lincoln made his position clear:

> . . . I think the authors of that notable instrument intended to include *all* men, but they did not intend to declare all men equal *in all respects*. . . . They did not mean to assert the obvious untruth, that all were then actually enjoying that equality, nor yet, that they were about to confer it immediately upon them. In fact they had no power to confer such a boon. They meant simply to declare the *right*, so that the *enforcement* of it might follow as fast as circumstances should permit. They meant to set up a standard maxim for free society, which should be familiar to all, and revered by all; constantly looked to, constantly labored for, and even though never perfectly attained, constantly approximated, and thereby constantly spreading and deepening its influence, and augmenting the happiness and value of life to all people of all colors everywhere.

On his way to Washington for his first inauguration, Lincoln stopped at Independence Hall in Philadelphia and made these impromptu remarks:

> I have never had a feeling politically that did not spring from the sentiments embodied in the Declaration of Independence. . . . I have often inquired of myself, what great principle or idea it was that kept this confederacy so long together. It was not the mere matter of the separation of the colonies from the mother land; but something in that Declaration giving liberty, not alone to the people of this country, but hope to the world for all future time. It was that which gave promise that in due time the

weights should be lifted from the shoulders of all men, and that *all* should have an equal chance. This is the sentiment embodied in that Declaration of Independence.

Yes, he personally felt the white race to be socially superior to races of color. Yes, he had argued in favor of relocation of the slaves to Africa upon the gradual, inevitable emancipation that would ultimately come from the playing out of economic and social forces, obviating the need for direct political intervention. Yes, he held off emancipating the slaves until two years into the Civil War when it became a military necessity. But also, yes, he always held slavery to be inherently evil and a flagrant violation of natural-born human rights. And he never shied away from publicly asserting this argument when the occasion demanded. And he came to recognize the worth and integrity of the brave black soldiers who took to the battlements in defense of his most precious ideal—the preservation and perpetuation of the Union.

Lincoln above all is the man who exposes the lie that human beings can only be moved by money. Truth, justice, civil harmony, education, literature, the life of the spirit—these were the principle motivating factors in Lincoln's life.

It is this wise, brave and sad Lincoln that I try to capture in my song. Borrowing the restless figure (and title) from the Vachel Lindsay poem, I'm looking for the Lincoln of all the people—who suffered with the mothers of the slain on the battlefields of the Civil War; the Lincoln who listened to the disenfranchised—Frederick Douglass among them—and left them with the knowledge that they had been heard; the Lincoln of our national poet, Walt Whitman, who in his grief at the President's assassination, penned perhaps the greatest American elegy:

> When lilacs last in the dooryard bloom'd,
> And the great star early droop'd in the western sky in the night,
> I mourned, and yet shall mourn with ever-returning spring.
>
> Ever-returning spring, trinity sure to me you bring,
> Lilac blooming perennial and drooping star in the west,
> And thought of him I love.
> O powerful western fallen star!
> O shades of night—O moody, tearful night!
> O great star disappear'd—O the black murk that hides the star!
> O cruel hands that hold me powerless—O helpless soul of me!
> O harsh surrounding cloud that will not free my soul. . . .

Words and Music
© 2009 by John Perrault

Abe Lincoln Walks at Midnight

Abe

Verse 1:

Lin- coln walks at mid-night   strolls the emp- ty streets

pass- es by the Court-house   where the pol- i- ti- cians meet

takes a turn   a- round the square a-round the elm— tree

looks up through the twist- ed limbs to the span-gled gal-a— xy.

Chorus 1:

I can see— his eyes   shin-ing,   flood-ing full of stars—

I can hear him   sigh-ing   in his sad- ness.

And I can see   the flag fly-ing   e-ven in   the dark   Abe

Lin-coln walks   at mid-night   and he's rest-less.   (repeat for Verse 2)

Abe Lincoln Walks at Midnight (continued)

Verse 3:

McDowell marching green recruits to the gray Manassas line,
orders to fix bayonets leave your packs behind
Beauregard comes charging at them now they're running blind—
Bull Run's been a raging river ever since this time.

Chorus 2:

I can see the sky darken cannon smoke and sparks and
I can hear the groaning of the dying.
I can see the rebels charging, all those Stars and Bars— and the
bloody field where the Union boys are lying.

Abe Lincoln Walks at Midnight

Lyrics

Abe Lincoln walks at midnight,
strolls the empty streets,
passes by the Courthouse
where the politicians meet—
takes a turn around the square,
around the Elm tree,
looks up through the twisted limbs
to the spangled galaxy.

Chorus 1:
And I can see his eyes shining,
flooding full of stars—
and I can hear him sighing in his sadness.
And I can see the flag flying
even in the dark—
Abe Lincoln walks at midnight and he's restless.

And he's got on his sable coat,
sable stove-pipe hat,
sloping shoulders, loping gait,
there's no one walks like that—
he's heading for the edge of town
where the troops are bivouacked,
and the moonlight on Manassas
glitters on the trampled grass.

Chorus 1: And I can see his eyes shining . . .

McDowell marching green recruits
to the gray Manassas line,
orders to *fix bayonets*
leave your packs behind—
Beauregard comes charging at them
now they're running blind—
Bull Run's been a raging river
ever since this time.

Chorus 2:
And I can see the sky darken,
cannon smoke and sparks—
and I can hear the groaning of the dying—

And I can see the rebels charging,
all those Stars and Bars—
and the bloody field where the Union boys are lying.

Battle of the Seven Days,
Lee and George McClellan,
slashing, cursing, shells bursting,
just outside of Richmond—
cross the Rappahannock River
Bull Run to Antietam,
soldiers falling filling ditches—
half way up to heaven.

Chorus 2: And I can see the sky darken . . .

And here's a boy of sixteen years,
jacket navy blue,
a splash of red upon his chest
where the bullet made it through—
and Lincoln holds him in his arms
the way that mothers do,
the last full measure of devotion
wrapped around those two.

How strange it seems for any man
asking God's assistance,
to wring his bread out of the sweat
of another man's existence—
but let us judge not carelessly
lest there be no deliverance,
till every drop of blood by lash
be paid for our offences.

Abe Lincoln, rail splitter,
pleads the Constitution:
The Union is our sacred goal,
it is not abolition—
Right makes might, he likes to say,
go read the Declaration,
winds up freeing all the slaves
in the great Emancipation.

One hundred thousand black men
now join the Northern cause,
Lincoln seeing how they fight

and suffer gives him pause—
he watches blacks in navy blue
turn freedom warriors:
All men are equal, that's the truth,
I always said it was.

Little town of Gettysburg,
Cemetery Ridge,
so many soldiers buried here
it's now our heritage—
Lincoln walks this hallowed ground,
he makes his pilgrimage:
This field we cannot consecrate,
that's a soldier's privilege.

Chorus 1: And I can see his eyes shining . . .

There stands General George McClellan
just outside his tent,
Lincoln looking hard at him
there's been an argument—
and there goes General Henry Halleck,
here comes General Grant,
Save the Union, Lincoln orders,
That's our covenant.

Chorus 2: And I can see the sky darken . . .

Sherman marching to the sea,
Schofield smashing Hood,
Grant attacking Petersburg,
the country soaked in blood—
Appomattox Court House
can the War be done for good?
If grace be shed upon these dead
will grace bless brotherhood?

Chorus 3:
And I can see surrender breaking
terrible swift swords,
and I can hear the generals agonizing—
and I can see the soldiers staking
crosses in the sward,
in the killing fields where a smoky haze is rising.

Theater box all dark tonight,
time for the assassin,
Lincoln's life left on the stage
to play out every Passion—
But he from whom all blessings flow
must never be forgotten,
when lilacs bloom around your door
you can't ignore Abe Lincoln.

Chorus 1: And I can see his eyes shining . . .

Frederick Douglass

FREDERICK DOUGLASS

Born— Circa February, 1817, Talbot County, Maryland

Youth— Life with Grandmother Betsy, Lloyd's Plantation, Auld's Home, Baltimore, St. Michaels, Mr. Covey's discipline

Maturity— Escape to New Bedford, abolition work, publication of *The North Star*, recruitment of black soldiers, consultations with the President, Consul General to Haiti; Significant writings: Rochester Ladies' Anti-Slavery Society (1852); Oration on Unveiling of Freedmen's Monument, Washington, D.C. (1876), Speech at Elmira (1880), *Life and Times of Frederick Douglass* (1881)

Words— "I have said that President Lincoln was a white man and shared towards the colored race the prejudices common to his countrymen. Looking back to his times and to the condition of his country, we are compelled to admit that this unfriendly feeling on his part may be safely set down as one element of his wonderful success in organizing the loyal American people for the tremendous conflict before them. . . . His great mission was to accomplish two things: first, to save his country from dismemberment and ruin; and second, to free his country from the great crime of slavery. . . . Had he put the abolition of slavery before the salvation of the Union, he would have inevitably driven from him a powerful class of the American people and rendered resistance to rebellion impossible. . . ."

—Freedmen's Monument Oration

Died— February 20, 1895, Cedar Hill, Washington, D.C.

"The Ballad of Frederick Douglass"

Douglass was born to a black slave woman and an anonymous white father on the Eastern Shore of Maryland in 1817. Subsequently placed by his grandmother on Colonel Lloyd's estate in Talbot County, his life appeared headed for one of submission and toil in the gulag of the great slave plantations of the South. But the inner fire of his human spirit was kindled by certain experiences he took to heart at a very young age: At seven he witnessed a good deal of brutality inflicted on slaves at Colonel Lloyd's, sufficient to make him wonder: "Why am I a slave? Why are some people slaves and others masters?" By the time he was nine, he was comparing himself to the blackbirds, "in whose wild and sweet songs I fancied them so happy. Their apparent joy only deepened the shades of my sorrow. . . . I was just as well aware of the unjust, unnatural, and murderous character of slavery, when nine years old, as I am now."

At the age of ten he was sent to the Aulds of Baltimore, where he learned to read—taught by his mistress Sophia and by certain white street urchins who helped him with his letters. The great orator, editor and author later relates in his autobiography that listening to Master Hugh Auld scold his wife for teaching the boy to read, he gleaned the significance of just what literacy could mean. He quotes Auld as follows:

> "Learning will spoil the best nigger in the world. If he learns to read the Bible it will forever unfit him to be a slave. He should know nothing but the will of his master, and learn to obey it. As to himself, learning will do him no good, but a great deal of harm, making him disconsolate and unhappy. If you teach him to read, he'll want to write, and this accomplished, he'll be running away with himself."

Douglass wasn't cowed by his master's outburst. Picking up change by blacking boots, he managed to purchase a schoolbook, *The Columbian Orator*, and was taken by political speeches of great historical figures touching on freedom. And, as we see from his personal testimony, freeing the mind leads to thinking about freedom itself. Douglass is living testimony to the fact that ideas have consequences. And that freedom to a slave doesn't mean money.

Douglass finally broke the bonds of his chains by an audacious sprint for freedom in 1838. Eventually conscripted for the abolitionist campaign by William Lloyd Garrison and others, he traveled to England, Scotland, and Ireland to advance the cause and avoid arrest. One of the critical things he learned early on was the concrete significance of the words of the Declaration of Independence. How could Jefferson have been serious if human beings of color were not recognized as possessing the same "unalienable rights" as those of the white race? Writing from Glasgow to Horace Greeley in 1846, he confronted the contradiction directly:

> An aged anti-slavery gentleman in Dublin, with whom I had the honor several times to dine during my stay in that city, has the Declaration of Independence and a number of the portraits of the distinguished founders of the American Republic. He bought them many years ago, in token of his admiration of the men and their principles. But, said he, after speaking of the sentiments of the Declaration—looking up as it hung in a costly frame—I am often tempted to turn its face to the wall, it is such a palpable contradiction of the spirit and practices of the American people at this time.

And after returning to the United States, he dramatically hammered the point home in his speech to the Rochester Ladies' Anti-Slavery Society, July 5, 1852:

> . . . The 4th of July is the first great fact in your nation's history—the very ring-bolt in the chain of your yet undeveloped destiny. . . . I have said that the Declaration of Independence is the ring-bolt to the chain of your nation's destiny; so, indeed, I regard it. The principles contained in that instrument are saving principles. Stand by those principles, be true to them on all occasions, in all places, against all foes, and at whatever cost. . . .
>
> Fellow-citizens, pardon me, allow me to ask, why am I called upon to speak here to-day? What have I, or those I represent, to do with your national independence? Are the great principles of political freedom and of natural justice, embodied in that Declaration of Independence, extended to us? And am I, therefore, called upon to bring our humble offering to the national altar, and to confess the benefits and express devout gratitude for the blessings resulting from your independence to us?

Would to God, both for your sakes and ours, that an affirmative answer could be truthfully returned to these questions! Then would my task be light, and my burden easy and delightful. For who is there so cold, that a nation's sympathy could not warm him? Who so obdurate and dead to the claims of gratitude, that would not thankfully acknowledge such priceless benefits? Who so stolid and selfish, that would not give his voice to swell the hallelujahs of a nation's jubilee, when the chains of servitude had been torn from his limbs? I am not that man. In a case like that, the dumb might eloquently speak, and the "lame man leap as an hart."

But, such is not the state of the case. I say it with a sad sense of the disparity between us. I am not included within the pale of this glorious anniversary! Your high independence only reveals the immeasurable distance between us. The blessings in which you, this day, rejoice, are not enjoyed in common. The rich inheritance of justice, liberty, prosperity and independence, bequeathed by your fathers, is shared by you, not by me. The sunlight that brought life and healing to you, has brought stripes and death to me. This Fourth [of] July is yours, not mine.

In 1863, Douglass was received at the White House by President Lincoln. Two giants meeting for the first time—both born in poverty, self-educated, ambitious, proud, and bent on advancing the principles stated in the Declaration. Douglass was not happy with the President's goal of Union first and foremost, even if it meant allowing slavery to continue in those rebelling states that would lay down their arms.

Upon entering the visitor's room, Douglass was immediately put at ease by the "great man." Douglass's immediate purpose was to raise the issue of unequal treatment of black troops in the Federal Army, which he did directly with the President. Lincoln listened intently to his three specific complaints: disparity of wages, lack of protection for black recruits captured by rebels, and failure to promote deserving black soldiers. Lincoln made no bones about the facts—he had, he argued, to deal with a deep-seated national prejudice against people of color, and the fact there were any black soldiers at all was a huge step in advancing the interests of black Americans. He suggested that equality in wages would inevitably arrive over time. Nor did he agree that revenging atrocities committed by rebels against black soldiers by having Union forces commit them themselves would deter the bloodshed. But he concurred with Douglass that any deserving soldier, white or black, should be promoted in rank and promised he would see to it that any soldier of color commended to him by his secretary of war would receive a commission.

Douglass did not agree with everything he heard, but nonetheless he came away with a sense of the honesty, integrity and anguish of the embattled President and decided to continue to enlist black recruits to serve the Union.

Douglass was invited back to the White House again, this time to discuss with the President the best way to bring southern slaves within the Federal lines. Lincoln was being pressured from powerful northern factions to make peace at the earliest opportunity, and should his hand be forced in this direction, he sought to have as many slaves safely in liberated territory as possible. The Emancipation Proclamation would free only those slaves still held in bondage by rebelling states. If a negotiated settlement were to occur, their status would be placed in jeopardy. In his autobiography, Douglass expresses his amazement at the President's passion for securing freedom for his people:

> He saw the danger of premature peace, and, like a thoughtful and sagacious man as he was, wished to provide means of rendering such consummation as harmless as possible. I was the more impressed by this benevolent consideration because he before said, in answer to the peace clamor, that his object was to *save the Union*, and to do so with or without slavery. What he said on this day showed a deeper moral conviction against slavery than I had ever seen before in anything spoken or written by him.

In this ballad I am primarily relying on Douglass's accounting of his own life, in the revised 1892 edition of *The Life and Times of Frederick Douglass*. To read Douglass is to get inside the reality of slavery. And Douglass recognized the fundamental importance of the songs of the slaves in coming to grips with that reality:

> The songs of the slaves represented their sorrows, rather than their joys. Like tears, they were a relief to aching hearts. It is not inconsistent with the constitution of the human mind that it avails itself of one and the same method for expressing opposite emotions. Sorrow and desolation have their songs, as well as joy and peace.

Words and Music
© 2009 by John Perrault

The Ballad of Frederick Douglass

The Ballad of Frederick Douglass

Lyrics

What's my heart doing banging these bars?
What's my back doing wearing these scars?
Up in the sky—blackbirds flying—
Clouds dragging chains over me.

Chorus:
Clouds dragging chains over me (× 2)
Clouds dragging chains, who remembers my name?
(Clouds dragging chains over me.)—(implied)

What's my name, where's my body belong?
Where's Mama—Granny—all gone?
Talbot County, Eastern Shore, I was born— Lord—Clouds *dragging* . . .

Captain Anthony's boss for Colonel Lloyd,
Captain's the man to avoid—
Running Lloyd's estate, whip a slave for one mistake—Clouds *dragging* . . .

Aunty Esther getting whipped for kissing Ned,
Aunty—Captain keeps her for his bed—
Aunty's heart hurt—bleeding through her shirt—Clouds *dragging* . . .

Overseer drives a slave like a horse,
Overseer Austin Gore he's the worst—
Bill Denby stood his ground, Gore shot him down—Clouds *dragging* . . .

Oh the heart's got no language like a song,
Let the heart sing, the heart will be strong—
Slave song glad? underneath it's sad—Clouds *dragging* . . .

Chorus: Clouds *dragging* . . .

They put me on a boat for Baltimore,
I'm maybe nine or ten, not much more—
Miss Sophia, Master Hugh, take me in, give me shoes—Clouds *dragging* . . .

Miss Sophia treats me so nice—
Miss Sophia teaching me to read and write—
Master Hugh in a rage—rips away the page—Clouds *dragging* . . .

Mr. Covey come to whip me till I break—
Mr. Covey I'm a man make no mistake—
Mr. Covey knocks me down, I pin him to the ground—Clouds *dragging* . . .

I'm on the run—1838—
Black sailor gives me papers to escape—
Freedom or the grave, run for it slave—Clouds *dragging* . . .

September third, I never will forget,
Heart pounding like a hammer in my chest—
Make the train at Baltimore, Philadelphia, New York—Clouds *breaking* . . .

Chorus: Clouds *breaking chains* . . .

The *Liberator* is my paper, is my voice:
Free the slaves! Moral man has no choice—
In New Bedford on the docks, careful with that talk—Clouds *breaking* . . .

Mr. Garrison puts me on the stage,
Tell the world what it's like for a slave—
I teach the bloody facts—the lessons on my back—Clouds *breaking* . . .

The Declaration says that I am a man,
The Declaration Mr. Lincoln defends—
Right makes might—Jefferson was right—Clouds *breaking* . . .

Captain Brown planning Harpers Ferry raid,
Captain Brown tries his best to persuade—
John Brown's a noble man, but this raid's a crazy plan—Clouds *breaking* . . .

Mr. Lincoln thinking hard on the war,
Mr. Lincoln thinking Union is his cause—
No Mr. Lincoln, it's emancipation—Clouds *breaking* . . .

Chorus: Clouds breaking . . .

John Booth fingering his gun,
John Booth—know what you've done?
You've acted out the play, they still put on today—Clouds *dragging* . . .

Jim Crow smiling in my face,
Jim Crow slandering my race—
Exercise your vote, wind up on a rope—Clouds *dragging* . . .

Wonder if Aunty Esther's in the fields,
Wonder if Aunty's cooking meals—
Still see Aunty stripped, Captain with his whip—Clouds *dragging* . . .

Don't know if Mama's in the ground—
Don't know if Granny's looking down—
Back in Talbot County, Lloyd's got all the money—Clouds *dragging* . . .

Rocking on my porch at Cedar Hill,
Looking out across my Country still—
Think you can't go on? Come on up, we'll talk some—Clouds *breaking* . . .

Chorus: Clouds *breaking chains* . . .

Elizabeth Cady Stanton

ELIZABETH CADY STANTON

Born—   November 12, 1815, Johnstown, New York

Youth—   Private schooling; Denied entrance to University due to
              gender; Matriculated Troy Female Seminary; Law study
              with father

Maturity—   Involvement with Temperance and Abolition Movements;
              marriage to Abolitionist Henry Stanton; Women's Rights
              Convention, Seneca Falls, 1848; with Susan B. Anthony
              founded American Equal Rights Association (1866), *The
              Revolution* (1868), and the National Woman Suffrage
              Association (1869); Significant writings: "The Solitude of
              Self"; Introduction and contributions to *The Woman's Bible*

Words—   "We hold these truths to be self-evident; that all men and
              women are created equal . . . "
                   —*Declaration of Sentiments, Seneca Falls Convention
                          (with Lucretia Mott, Martha C. Wright,
                                  and Mary Ann McClintock.)*

Died—   October 26, 1902, New York City

"Call Me Cady Stanton"

Elizabeth Cady Stanton was the daughter of Daniel and Margaret Livingston Cady, born in Johnstown, New York, in 1815, two years before Douglass and Thoreau, five years before Tubman. Her father was a lawyer and judge who supported Elizabeth's educational ambitions even to the extent of training her in the law. Denied access to Union College in New York because of her sex, she matriculated at Troy Female Seminary, graduating in 1833. Thereafter, she returned to Johnstown where she took up various social causes that her education had awakened her to. Slavery was at the top of her agenda.

The question necessarily arises: how is it that a comfortable, socially respectable young woman in upstate New York came to be involved in the most volatile issues of the day? One apparent reason was her sister Tryphena's husband, Edward Bayard—learned, cultured, philosophically attuned to a better world. He played a prominent role in young Elizabeth's life, and ultimately wound up proposing to her when his wife was away. Another was her cousin, Gerrit Smith, the great philanthropist from Peterboro, New York, (son of Peter Smith, John Jacob Astor's partner in furs) who provided an intellectual wealth of progressive ideas. As a young woman Elizabeth had dabbled in religious, abolitionist and temperance activities. Encouraged by the philosophies of Bayard and Smith, she gradually realized that a life of social engagement and political action would be far more meaningful than one of security and comfort resting on wealth.

In 1840, Elizabeth Cady married the social activist, abolitionist, and writer, Henry Brewster Stanton, and accompanied him to London to attend the International Anti-Slavery Conference. There, two significant events took place: she met and befriended Lucretia Mott, a Quaker activist, and she was refused, along with Mott, a seat at the Conference. This positive/negative experience only served to fuel Cady Stanton's urgent conviction that the evil of slavery was directly connected to the oppression of women. If a portion of humanity felt entitled to enslave the black race, that same sense of entitlement fueled half of humanity to denigrate, control and suppress the other half. Consequently, Cady Stanton and Mott joined forces to fight these twin evils, dedicating themselves to the abolition of slavery and to the realization of full equality for women.

For Cady Stanton, Mott, and their associates, the transition from exclusively promulgating abolition to a wider demand for the full equality of women was a moral imperative. Unlike the slave masters and the male masters, they took Jefferson's Declaration of Independence seriously—and they insisted upon its inclusion of women. If the men couldn't or wouldn't see what that Declaration really meant, then the women would spell it out for them. In 1848 at Seneca Falls, New York, they organized the first women's rights convention in the United States. Three hundred participants showed up—mostly women, but a significant minority of men. Prominent speakers, including Mott, Cady Stanton, Frederick Douglass and Mary Ann McClintock addressed the audience. The "Declaration of Sentiments"—modeled on Jefferson's document, was read and approved by the attendees: "We hold these truths to be self-evident: that all men and women are created equal . . . "

Tracing Jefferson's language, Cady Stanton and co-authors Mott, Wright, and McClintock did not mince words: "The history of mankind is a history of repeated injuries and usurpations on the part of man toward woman, having in direct object the establishment of an absolute tyranny over her. . . ." Thus was born the feminist movement in the United States.

In the 1850s, Cady Stanton went on to forge another one of the great political alliances in American history—a more than fifty-year active association with Susan B. Anthony, the de-facto author of the Nineteenth Amendment to the United States Constitution. (The Amendment, which gave women the right to vote, had been urged upon Congress by Anthony's testimony every year from 1869 to the year of her death in 1906. It was finally adopted in 1920.) Arising out of their respective activities in support of the Temperance Movement, their bonding was the result of their mutual recognition that the fundamental political rights they were struggling for would never be fully realized until suffrage was granted to women as well as blacks.

Immediately after the Civil War, Cady Stanton and Anthony founded the American Equal Rights Association and, in due course, began publishing a progressive paper: *The Revolution*. Its masthead read: "Men, their rights, and nothing more; women, their rights, and nothing less." Despite risking opprobrium with her publication of *The Woman's Bible*, which severely criticized male-dominated religions, Cady Stanton forged on with her life's work for women's rights. And it wasn't long before that work ran into a solid wall of male resistance.

Cady Stanton came to see that her support of abolition and black suffrage was not being reciprocated by black and white leaders who refused to lobby for the inclusion of women in the Fifteenth Amendment—the Amendment which enfranchised the newly freed black male without mentioning women. Cady Stanton raised a mighty protest. This led to an unfortunate verbal exchange with Frederick Douglass at Steinway Hall in New York in 1869. It would be another six decades before the wounds then and there inflicted would begin to be seriously addressed—by the healing hand of Eleanor Roosevelt.

Perhaps Cady Stanton's most deeply felt writing was an address she delivered before the Judiciary Committee of the House of Representatives in 1892. Titled "The Solitude of Self," she argued that all human beings are equal because each one of us is ultimately alone:

> The strongest reason for giving woman all the opportunities for higher education, for the full development of her faculties, her forces of mind and body; for giving her the most enlarged freedom of thought and action; a complete emancipation from all forms of bondage, of custom, dependence, superstition; from all the crippling influences of fear—is the solitude and personal responsibility of her own individual life. . . . We come into the world alone, unlike all who have gone before us, we leave it alone, under circumstances peculiar to ourselves. . . .

Six thousand people attended her eightieth birthday at the Metropolitan Opera in New York. There she reminded her audience of how strongly she had been warned not to involve herself with the Seneca Falls crowd back in 1848. How that radical course would only result in her ridicule and social isolation. Those who did the warning we do not remember. We do, however, remember Elizabeth Cady Stanton. She died eighteen years short of the day women could finally vote.

Jefferson's Dream
JOHN
PERRAULT

Words and Music
© 2009 by John Perrault

Call Me Cady Stanton

Call Me Cady Stanton

Lyrics

Chorus:
Oh my name is Cady Stanton,
I'm Elizabeth to my friends,
I'm not one to be discouraged or be cowed.

I stood up with Douglass
For all Black Americans,
And he stands up with me for every woman now.

Oh the pace of that woman, it was daunting—
In her face, not a trace of compromise—
With Susan Anthony, some fifty years and counting—
Cady made the case for women's rights.

"I've read the law, my father was a lawyer—
I know all the ways they sabotaged the blacks—
1840, at the Anti-Slavery Conference—
They made Lucretia Mott and me go sit in back."

"I ask: for whom did we fight the Revolution?
I ask: who gets to claim the answer's, 'man'?
Now ask yourself: when you read the Constitution—
How come half of us are missing from the plan?"

"You say God says it somewhere in the Bible—
You say Women all are libel to His Law—
But Scripture says Man himself is just as libel—
And God knows what Scripture's really for."

"We hold these truths, like Jefferson before us—
We write large because his writing was so small—
Seneca Falls—our Declaration proves us:
Men and Women, equal rights, for one and all."

(*repeat chorus*)

Henry David Thoreau

HENRY DAVID THOREAU

Born—   July 12, 1817, Concord, Massachusetts

Youth—   Wood walks, chores, pencils, Harvard

Maturity—   Teacher, lecturer, Emerson disciple, Walden, surveyor,
writer; Significant writings: *A Week on the Concord
and Merrimack*; *Walden*; *Civil Disobedience*; "Slavery in
Massachusetts"; "Plea for Captain John Brown."

Words—   "When first I took up my abode in the woods . . . on the
Fourth of July, 1845, my house was not finished for winter. . . .
I went to the woods because I wished to live deliberately,
to front only the essential facts of life, and see if I could
not learn what it had to teach, and not, when I came to die,
discover that I had not lived. . . . I wanted to live deep and
suck out all the marrow of life . . . and, if it proved to be
mean, why then to get the whole and genuine meanness of it,
and publish its meanness to the world; or if it were sublime,
to know it by experience . . . "   —*Walden*

Died—   May 6, 1862, Concord, Massachusetts

"Thoreau on Thoreau"

What does Thoreau have to offer us besides trips to the pond and paeans to turtles' eggs? Besides a comic look at his Concord neighbors wrapping economic chains around their legs? His two-year sojourn, commencing in 1845 at Walden Woods, is embedded in our cultural consciousness. It stands for the primacy of the individual and the dignity of self-determination. Born in 1817 in Concord, Massachusetts, his was a life of non-cooperation with the evils of organization. The stupidity of government. He would be alone and left alone. What did it matter that man made a slave of man—both black and white? There was no surprise in the finding. Reformers were wasting everybody's time. Only the individual could reform himself, as his now famous "Civil Disobedience" makes perfectly plain.

But then—as if out of the smoke from some backwoods chimney—comes "Slavery in Massachusetts" in 1854. And five years later, his two lectures in sympathy with John Brown. What has happened? Henry never let the Mexican War work him up to the pitch that the 1850 Fugitive Slave Act did. Here is righteous wrath and political outrage. Henry enters the public stage on a public matter.

The Mexican War was the doing of the Federal Government. It was far away, down on the border. It was a corrupting fever that could be left to infect what and whom it would and run itself out. For all its contagion, Henry was safe in the woods. But the Slave Act—that was another matter entirely. If not so much for the abomination that he considered the institution to be, then for the fact it made Massachusetts—and himself—complicit! And had he not, on occasion, when circumstances were ripe, helped in small ways to hasten the fugitive slave north to Canada? To do so now would make him subject to prosecution for a crime! Would actually impinge on the freedom of his own conscience by demanding he turn the slave in!

As consistently insistent on ignoring the government as he was, here was the government stepping into his house. His home. His heart and soul. Henry would have none of it. It brought him to his feet in a speech decrying how he had "lost" his country for what it was doing. A country he had never directly recognized to have meaning for him in the past. Now there were political things worth fighting for. Now he might be forced to put his life on the line in opposition to an intolerable social evil. So, in 1859, he presents his "Plea for Captain John Brown" and says:

> I pity the poor in bondage that have none to help them; that is why I am here; not to gratify any personal animosity, revenge, or vindictive spirit. It is my sympathy with the oppressed and the wronged, that are as good as you, and as precious in the sight of God. . . . I want you to understand that I respect the rights of the poorest and weakest of colored people, oppressed by the slave power, just as much as I do those of the most wealthy and powerful. . . . I wish to say, furthermore, that you had better, all you people at the South, prepare yourselves for a settlement of that question, that must come up for settlement sooner than you are prepared for it. The sooner you are prepared the better. You may dispose of me very easily. I am nearly disposed of now; but this question is still to be settled,— this negro question, I mean; the end of that is not yet.

Thoreau closes with a vision of the fulfillment of the Declaration of Independence:

> I foresee the time when the painter will paint that scene, no longer going to Rome for a subject; the poet will sing it; the historian record it; and, with the Landing of the Pilgrims and the Declaration of Independence, it will be the ornament of some future national gallery, when at least the present form of Slavery shall be no more here. We shall then be at liberty to weep for Captain Brown. Then, and not till then, we will take our revenge.

And it was less than two months after this speech that Thoreau was indeed put to the test. When Jackson Merriam, one of Brown's cohorts, appeared in Concord after the raid at Harper's Ferry, Thoreau, with a horse borrowed from Emerson, took him to the station to escape north to Canada.

Even Thoreau—the supreme individualist—recognized that there are times that try men's souls to the point of social action—social responsibility. We don't remember him primarily for that—but we can't deny he climbed the stairs to that trembling platform when it counted.

Words and Music
© 2009 by John Perrault

Thoreau on Thoreau

Thoreau on Thoreau

Lyrics

"Henry D." they call me, when it's time to go to church,
on the only day that they don't say that it's time to go to work,
but work for them means pencils, and you know pencils—I just can't—
my kind of work is out in nature's manufacturing plant.

My father's was a shop keep, before those pencils won,
in July of 1817, I became my father's son;
I grew up exploring Concord, I've got Concord in my blood—
I canoed and swam the river by the rude arch that spans the flood.

Chorus:
David Henry, Henry D., oh it's good to see you back—
It's been so long since Walden Pond, since your living in a one-room shack.
Let's get you down those hiking shoes, Cape Cod and Maine—how's that?
A birch canoe and a book or two for the Concord and the Merrimack.
For the Concord and the Merrimack.

I went out to Walden Woods to live life to the bone,
suck the marrow out of it, deliberately, alone;
I see men in desperation, I see ladies in distress—
I went to the woods to confront the facts and raise a little consciousness.

Consciousness—that's a funny word—it was beans I raised in fact;
watching them poke up through the dirt, well that's quite a conscious act—
Simplicity! Simplicity! What is it that you really want?
Just enough to eat and good night's sleep and a roof for the bats to haunt.

I spent most nights just listening to the hounds and how they'd howl,
to the little creatures scuttling, to the wing beats of an owl;
listening and looking out and waking up my eyes
to the sleep of all my countrymen, just snoring away their lives.

Oh I know they say I'm ornery, I'm not one much for fun;
I don't drink but I can dance and I know how to handle a gun—
I'd like to think that trying to think can make a satisfying life,
and I can love, but I won't say who, even if I don't have a wife.

Chorus: David Henry, Henry D . . .

I strolled to town one afternoon and I found myself in jail,
seems I hadn't paid my polling tax, (I'm a white Anglo-Saxon male);
Ralph Waldo comes to the window, he says: "Henry—you in there?"
I strained my eyes, it was quite a surprise, I said: "Ralph, what you doing out there?"

I was born in this democracy, a majority of one;
I hope to make my way in life without stepping on anyone—
You stand for abolition? You're against this Mexican War?
Then you've got no choice, you've got to raise your voice, what else is conscience for?

You don't cooperate with evil—to me it's just common sense.
I wrote all about it in a book they call, *Civil Disobedience*;
Leave me alone, I leave you alone—but the law won't let us be—
The Fugitive Slave Law's what I mean, and it's staining our country.

If we've got to have a government, then let it govern right,
let a man be first a man before politicians get a hold of his life—
The Declaration makes the case—I won't tear Jefferson down—
But I look to the day when there's no more slaves and we can mourn for Captain Brown.

Chorus: David Henry, Henry D . . .

I tune my flute to the western wind, to the universal key;
they say the music of the spheres makes quite a harmony—
I'll take you in my birch canoe, we'll paddle all the way to Mars,
drag our feet in the gravel bed of those grainy, mystical stars.

"Henry D." (they're calling me), "it's time to go to bed.
Time to put that pen back down, pull the covers up over your head."
But covers for them mean sheets to sleep, and white sheets—I just can't—
My kind of cover is colored green out in nature's manufacturing plant.

Chorus: David Henry, Henry D . . .

Ida B. Wells

IDA B. WELLS

Born—   July 16, 1862, Holly springs, Mississippi

Youth—   Slavery, orphaned at fourteen, mother to her siblings

Maturity—   Teacher in Memphis, writer, newspaper publisher, political
                 activist, civil rights advocate; Significant writings: *Crusade
                 for Justice, The Autobiography of Ida B. Wells; A Red Record*

Words—   " . . . Those were precious days in which I sat at the feet
                 of this Pioneer . . . (Susan B. Anthony) in the work of
                 women's suffrage. She had endeavored to make me see
                 that for the sake of expediency one had often to stoop to
                 conquer on this color question. . . . She said when women
                 called their first convention back in 1848 . . . Frederick
                 Douglass . . . stood up with them. 'He said he could not
                 do otherwise; that we were among the friends who fought
                 his battles when he first came among us appealing for our
                 interest in the antislavery cause. From that day until the day
                 of his death Frederick Douglass was an honorary member
                 of the National Women's Suffrage Association. . . . But when
                 the Equal Suffrage Association went to Atlanta . . . I myself
                 asked Mr. Douglass not to come. I did not want to subject
                 him to humiliation, and I did not want anything to get in the
                 way of bringing the southern white women into our suffrage
                 association . . . And you think I was wrong in so doing?'
                 she asked. I answered uncompromisingly yes, for I felt that
                 although she may have made gains for suffrage, she had also
                 confirmed white women in their attitude of segregation."

                 —*Crusade for Justice*

Died—   March 25, 1931, Chicago

"Ida B. Wells—
The Lynching at the Curve"

Ida B. Wells was born the daughter of slaves in Holly Springs, Mississippi, in 1862. During Reconstruction, her father, a carpenter, became socially active in their small community and participated in the newly formed "Loyal League," a black political organization. Her mother and father were firm believers in education. Shaw University was established in Holly springs in 1866 for the advancement of the freed slave population. Over time, Ida, her mother, and her siblings all attended. In 1878, a yellow fever epidemic spread through the area taking her parents and youngest sister. Ida took on the responsibilities of raising her other five siblings and paid the rent by teaching in a local school. Taking summer courses at Fisk University and Lemoyne Institute, she became qualified to teach in Memphis, moved there, and taught for seven years.

On May 4, 1884, she was physically removed by three men from the "ladies car" on a Chesapeake and Ohio passenger train traveling on Tennessee tracks. Ida sued for damages and won in the trial court. Elated, and for the first time in her life, Ida submitted an article to a local church paper about the incident. (The Tennessee Supreme Court subsequently reversed the verdict.) So well received was it, that the editor asked for more, and so began her "Iola" column that eventually got picked up by other black newspapers across the country. And Ida's voice came up from the depths, deploring the discrimination and injustices experienced by her people.

In 1889, Ida became the editor of the black Memphis newspaper, *Free Speech*. Her editorials took on the white establishment for turning their backs on the freed blacks of Memphis. After criticizing the Memphis school board for the deplorable conditions of black public schools, she was fired from her teaching position. And then came the incident which provides the title to my ballad, "The Lynching at the Curve." In March of 1892, three of Ida's close friends, Thomas Moss, Calvin McDowell, and Henry Stewart, opened "The People's Grocery," across from a well-established white grocery on a busy Memphis thoroughfare. With the decline in black patronage, the white grocers were not pleased. Pressure mounted from the white community to close "The People's" store. Before long, a gang of white thugs invaded the new grocery, only to be met by gunfire which wounded three of them. Ida's three friends were hauled off to jail. The morning papers screamed at the outrage of black men shooting white men. That night a white mob dragged the three from their cells and summarily executed them at an intersection where the trolley tracks made a wide curve into town.

Ida turned to her searing pen. White Memphis justice was no justice—how can the blacks live in a community where they are murdered with impunity for standing up for their rights? She advocated a mass migration of blacks out of Memphis, and six thousand heeded the call. She argued for black boycotts of white businesses, and those businesses felt the pain of the loss. In future columns, after diligent investigation and research, she went on to rail not only against this lynching, but the hundreds of lynchings across the land which, if not explicitly condoned, were more than tolerated by the white establishment. Too often the white-controlled media whipped up a frenzy whenever a black was accused of a crime—especially if it involved a white woman.

Ida pointed out in blunt terms that the repeated justification of such atrocities—the defilement of white women by black men—was a lie. To the extent that there was any sexual mixing of the races, she suggested it was consensual. This claim so enraged the Memphis white establishment, that it resulted in the "Free Speech" offices and presses being destroyed by a white mob. Ida moved to Chicago.

Settled in the north and continuing to write, Ida inaugurated the first American Negro Women's Civic clubs in Chicago and Boston in 1893. She became active in the suffrage movement and worked with Susan B. Anthony with whom she had profound disagreements over the exclusion of black women and subordination of black issues. She also worked with Jane Addams, co-founder of Hull House, a settlement home for educating the working class in Chicago. Ida married prominent activist Chicago lawyer F. L. Barnett and took over his paper, *The Conservator*. The couple had four children, and Ida was a loving, no-nonsense, hands-on mother. But that didn't mean she could ignore the indignities suffered by her race. In 1909 she was one of the founders of the N.A.A.C.P, and in 1913 she established the first black woman's suffrage club, "The Alpha Suffrage Club." Despite her prestigious social position and her marriage to a successful attorney, Ida never succumbed to the notion that wealth and acquisitions were meaningful goals in life. Ida could not rest comfortably while others suffered. Justice was everything to her.

Ida saw the inseparable relationship between equality for blacks and equality for women. The marrow of the Declaration of Independence was embedded in her bones. She recognized, as did W. E. B. Dubois in his paper, *Crises*, that "every argument for Negro suffrage is an argument for women's suffrage, every argument for women's suffrage is an argument for Negro Suffrage; both are great moments in democracy." Although Ida could recognize and appreciate the fact that Susan B. Anthony was personally not a racist, she could not abide the public stance Anthony took with regard to the issue of race when it came to women's suffrage. Anthony, who had the full-hearted support of Frederick Douglass in her campaigns, requested his absence when the Suffrage Association met in Atlanta in 1894 for fear of alienating Southern women. Anthony gaveled down a proposed resolution that black women ought not be segregated in smoking cars on the nation's railroads at the women's Michigan convention in 1899. For Ida, these kinds of "tactical decisions" were not merely an issue of strategy. Blacks were being lynched. It was an issue of moral imperative: the rights to life and liberty and happiness for American blacks were being grossly violated. Her people were being mutilated, raped, and murdered. This was no time for compromise.

When the National Woman's Suffrage Association directed that all black women were to march in a black group at the end of the suffrage parade in Washington D.C. in 1913, Ida made clear her resolve that black women were equal to white women by marching proudly with the Illinois contingent. To the end of her life, she never ceased advocating for her people—both men and women. More than once, she risked her life for that cause.

The salute she received from Frederick Douglass that prefaces her 1895 study of lynchings in the United States, *A Red Record*, honors the major contribution of the writings of Ida B. Wells:

> ... Brave Woman! You have done your people and mine a service which can neither be weighed or measured. If the American conscience were only half alive, if the American church and clergy were only half Christianized, if American moral sensibility were not hardened by persistent infliction of outrage and crime against colored people, a scream of horror, shame, and indignation would rise to Heaven wherever your pamphlet shall be read.

Words and Music
© 2009 by John Perrault

The Lynching at the Curve

The Lynching at the Curve

Lyrics

Where is everybody? Where's Mr. Jefferson?
That boy off skedaddled after putting down, putting down his writing pen?
Where's that old Abe Lincoln and his disappearing Reconstruction plan?
Someone's got a rope around my people's neck again.

My name is Ida B. Wells, I'm just a plain American—
Proud to be a woman and proud of the color, color of my skin—
I was born in Mississippi moved up to Memphis to teach the children—
Someone's got a rope around my people's neck again.

Memphis was the spot that a lot of my people got to settle in—
Set ourselves to working hard and raising up our children just the best we can—
1892, that was a good year for all of us to begin—
Someone's got a rope around my people's neck again.

Bridge: Star—Tell me where is my star—On the flag of America—
Fluttering free . . . × 2

Moss, McDowell, Stewart—they were three of my very best friends—
Opened up a grocery right across the road from the white competition—
Thugs attacked, they fought back, got arrested, jailed, dragged out and
killed every one of them—
Someone's got a rope around my people's neck again.

I raced out, wrote up the story in the newspaper that I ran—
Free Speech was the paper—not afraid, not afraid to take a stand—
White folks look the other way while they're stringing up all our good men—
Someone's got a rope around my people's neck again.

I wrote about all the lynchings stretching out, stretching out across the land—
Mob broke in my office, smashed my presses and you know Memphis let them in—
I went up north and asked around: am I still not a citizen?
Someone's got a rope around my people's neck again.

Bridge: Star . . . etc.

Somehow now I'm an upstart making trouble acting masculine—
Not only am I black but I'm a woman, I'm a woman, oh yes I am—
Equality and liberty—what say you says the Declaration?
Someone's got a rope around my people' neck again.

Black men, my God, they're dying, women crying for their freedom—
Oppress the one, oppress them all—then justice, justice is a fiction—
Susan Anthony, yes we've got to get the vote but that includes
all us black women—
Someone's got a rope around my people's neck again.

(Repeat first verse.)

Bridge: Star . . . etc.

Eleanor Roosevelt

ELEANOR ROOSEVELT

Born—   October 11, 1884, New York City

Youth—   Orphaned at ten; schooled in England at Allenswood
                 Academy, headed by the feminist educator Marie Souvestre;
                 taught at Rivington Settlement House

Maturity—   Marriage to FDR, mother of six children, political wife,
                 independent activist, first lady, chairwoman of committee
                 drafting Universal Declaration of Human Rights; Significant
                 Writings: *It's Up to the Women*, 1933; *This I Remember*, 1949;
                 "My Day" syndicated newspaper column, 1935–1962

Words—   "As I look back at the work thus far of our Human Rights
                 Commission I realize that its importance is twofold. In the
                 first place, we have put into words some inherent rights.
                 Beyond that, we have found that the conditions of our
                 contemporary world require the enumeration of certain
                 protections which the individual must have if he is to
                 acquire a sense of security and dignity in his own person . . .
                 "It seems to me most important that the Declaration
                 be accepted by all member nations, not because they will
                 immediately live up to all of its provisions, but because they
                 ought to support the standards toward which the nations
                 must henceforward aim . . . "
                 —*"The Promise of Human Rights,"* Foreign Affairs, *April, 1948*

Died—   November 1962, New York City

"Eleanor Calling"

Eleanor Roosevelt was born into the Roosevelt family on October 11, 1884 in New York City. Daughter of Elliott and Anna Roosevelt, she was the niece of President Teddy Roosevelt and fifth cousin to her future husband and President, FDR. Her young world turned on an axis of money, prestige, and cultural superiority.

Eleanor's mother died when she was eight, and her adored father died two years later. She was raised in her early years by her grandmother, and educated in England during her teen years. She did not go to college and was largely self-educated. At the age of nineteen, she volunteered at Rivington Settlement house in Manhattan as a teacher.

When first engaged to FDR, Eleanor was a political innocent. Her future husband couldn't claim much of a political consciousness either. As newly-weds, their concerns were primarily those of family and social life. Franklin was an indifferent law student struggling to graduate and Eleanor was a young bride looking to have a family.

By the time FDR became a New York State senator, Eleanor had her hands full with children and household. She was also undergoing a personal crisis, as she felt her life not measuring up to her potential. There was something deep in Eleanor's make-up that made her long to reach out to others and become engaged with the wider world. The more Franklin became enmeshed in political life, the more Eleanor's longing to involve herself in larger issues. Economic security and social position were not ends for her—they were the means by which she might do good in the world.

Franklin eventually was appointed Assistant Secretary of the Navy in the Wilson Administration. Eleanor's sense of purpose took on new urgency. She found that supporting her husband's endeavors and entertaining his colleagues and political associates led her to new ideas and provided her with an appreciation for the way the world of power worked. She became an avid reader in order to keep up. Reading led to questions, questions to actions. She opened her mind and heart to progressive thinkers who raised the call for action. She joined other women—and a few men—in challenging the status quo. Inadequate educational opportunity, poverty, urban decay, spousal abuse, child abuse, dangerous working conditions, economic discrimination against women, militancy, racial bigotry—all provoked Eleanor's wrath. She became the most prominent spokesperson for the marginalized, the brutalized, the neglected, in the first half of the American twentieth century.

What makes an affluent woman of significant social standing and comfortable prospects become involved with the plight of the toiling masses? With issues of international peace and social justice? When we consider how, over time, Eleanor became deeply committed to the major issues of her day, we can only marvel at her energy, passion and faith in human progress.

At the age of 19 she taught at the Rivington Street Settlement House in New York, and shortly thereafter became a researcher for the Consumers' League, investigating working conditions in factories and stores in New York. Her more progressive colleagues introduced her to the work and teachings of such women activists as Jane Addams and Carrie Cat Chapman, and she came to revere and support their work. After her marriage to FDR, she gradually became involved with a number of socially and economically active groups, including The Junior League, Rose Schneiderman's Women's Trade Union League, The League of Women Voters, The Association to Promote Proper Housing for Girls, the Bureau of Women's Activities of the Democratic National Committee, and The Foreign Policy Association. She helped to administer The Bok Peace Award, and worked to support legislation to protect child workers and to provide women with health care, including clinics for maternity and pediatric services.

As First Lady, she remained publicly active in dozens of causes that she passionately believed in—from world peace, to economic justice, to racial harmony. Perhaps her most significant contributions came in her role as writer. After touring Morgantown, West Virginia, an area so ravaged by the negligence and cruelty of mining operators that had mined it out and left it with dust, slag, poison, and filth to rot back into the hills, Eleanor wrote a blistering article in the *Women's Democratic News* to alert the world to the degradation she had witnessed. In 1936 she commenced one of the most popular syndicated columns of all time, "My Day," in which she candidly spoke to the American public about fundamental issues of concern—from baby care to world peace.

The evolution of her sense of purpose in the world was inextricably connected to her dismay at the ingrained inertia, pride, pragmatism, and culpable ignorance of political leaders of all stripes who failed to measure up to their responsibilities. And a major responsibility, in Eleanor's view, was for leaders to educate themselves on the problems at hand, face facts, draw up plans, and take action—all in the service of justice and human dignity.

It took Eleanor years to realize this about herself—that she cared so deeply for her fellow man she couldn't stand silent when justice cried out for action. She couldn't bear to see people marginalized, ignored, deprived of basic needs, oppressed, violated. She came to realize that racial bigotry and misogyny were cuts from the same tree—rotten at the core.

Not "sympathetic," but "empathetic" was how the great American journalist Vernon Jarrett described her concern. Who would know better than he? From the 1940s to 2004, the year he died, Jarrett was on the front lines covering the nation's racial divide and promoting the cause of racial equality. He was not blind to the speeches she gave in support of civil rights. He took note of how Eleanor had resigned from the D.A.R. in protest of their denial of Constitution Hall to the great black American singer Marian Anderson—and how she worked behind the scenes to arrange Anderson's famed concert at the Lincoln Memorial on Easter Day, 1939. He was witness to the public affection and appreciation Eleanor showed for Mary Mcleod Bethune, "First Lady of the Struggle," founder of Bethune-Cookman College, and president of the National Council of Negro Women. It was through Eleanor's intercession and encouragement that Bethune became director of Negro Affairs in the National Youth Administration during FDR's presidency.

Eleanor worked with Walter White, executive director of the N.A.A.C.P, to lobby FDR on supporting anti-lynching legislation. If it was a hard sell, it was not for their lack of trying. Associating herself with White was not politically advantageous, since he was a strong vocal advocate for protection of blacks from mob rule. Powerful people in Congress opposed him—the southern interests despised him—and FDR would not back him. Eleanor persevered with White nonetheless.

Eleanor was white, rich, privileged and powerful—yet Mr. Jarrett asserts unequivocally that the black community came to see it had a friend in the White House in Eleanor Roosevelt.

Eleanor grieved deeply on the death of her husband—but she did not retreat to the comfort of her home and family. Instead, she asserted herself more deeply in the causes to which she was so profoundly committed. President Truman appointed her as delegate to the U.N. Committee on Human Rights. She was soon elected chairwoman. The State Department made clear to her that the American Declaration of Independence should be the quiet paradigm for her work. Eleanor played the critical role of facilitating the drafting and confirmation of the Universal Declaration of Human Rights, despite the obstructive tactics of representatives from Russia and a few of the Soviet Republics. Members of her own delegation at times attempted to thwart her advocacy of a full human rights agenda. Eleanor would not be cowed. Nor would she take umbrage. What she would do is patiently work with resisting forces until accommodation could be reached with language everyone could accept. For Eleanor, scoring moral or ideological points was not the answer. Rather, productive results were the goal in furthering human rights.

And how did she conceive of human rights? The golden rule would not be too simple an answer: treat others as you would have others treat you. No complex academic theorizing necessary here. People need to live—therefore, they are entitled to food, shelter, and security as a matter of basic justice and common sense. From these basic physical considerations, certain conceptual requirements necessarily flow: people must be treated with dignity and respect. There is absolutely no justification for oppressing or discriminating against any individual, group or nation on the grounds of gender, religious beliefs, racial makeup, cultural values or ethnicity. People must be at liberty to support themselves and fulfill their aspirations. Eleanor's passionate concern for Jewish refugees after World War II—her behind-the-scenes work on their behalf, and her ultimate support for a two-state solution in Palestine—is testament to her recognition that practical action is required if basic human rights are to be realized.

Words and Music
© 2009 by John Perrault

Eleanor Calling

Eleanor Calling

Lyrics

Hello out there it's Eleanor here
Thought we'd have a little chat,

"My Day's" on the air
And dare I say that I regret

Not seeing more of you,
You and you,
Sweet people I can never forget—

For helping me through what I had to do,
It's not over yet.

Chorus:
It's not over yet. Well it's not over yet.
For helping me through what I had to do,
It's not over yet.

When first I went to the Settlements
I was a young aristocrat,

Jane Addams was just a name to me,
A name—imagine that,

She got me to speak my peace
For a world of peace
And women in politics—

Men and women, don't you see?
That it's not over yet.

Chorus: It's not over yet . . . etc.

Thanks to my love Franklin
I became a real democrat,

When controversy bridled him
I rode on up ahead

And when Miss Marian
Yes, Anderson,
Sang on the Lincoln steps—

To the massive crowd: "America"
I said it's not over yet.

Chorus: It's not over yet . . . etc.

Thanks to Walter White
I realized the plight of blacks,

For the first time in my life
I got a look behind the mask

And I saw all those lynchings,
Yes lynchings,
I just couldn't turn my back—

Now I'm talking with Dr. King
And it's not over yet.

Chorus: It's not over yet . . . etc.

When Franklin died I cried and cried
God knows I was upset,

God knows I tried to ride
It out with him and yes we kept up

Appearances,
Our differences,
Were more than I could ever accept—

My shining prince—my life since?
It's not over yet.

Chorus: It's not over yet . . . etc.

And that crusty Harry Truman
Made me a UN diplomat,

I wove Jefferson
Into the Universal Declaration:

Human Rights,
Equal rights,
Self-evident in fact—

We hold tyrants to these truths
And it's not over yet.

Chorus: It's not over yet . . . etc.

Permissions

The images of the eight Americans presented were made available by the following organizations:

Thomas Jefferson: Courtesy of the Library of Congress, LC-USZ62-53985

Harriet Tubman: Courtesy of the Library of Congress, LC-USZ62-7816

Abraham Lincoln: Courtesy of the Library of Congress, LC-DIG-ppmsca-19469

Frederick Douglass: Courtesy of the Library of Congress, LC-USZ62-15887

Elizabeth Cady Stanton: Courtesy of the Library of Congress, LC-USZ62-28195

Henry David Thoreau: Courtesy of the Library of Congress, LC-USZ61-361

Ida B. Wells: Courtesy of the Library of Congress, LC-USZ62-107756

Eleanor Roosevelt: Paris, UN, Nov. 1951, Courtesy of the Franklin D. Roosevelt Library, Digital Archives

The Eleanor Roosevelt quote on page 68 is reprinted by permission of *Foreign Affairs*, April, 1948, copyright (2009) by the Council on Foreign Relations, Inc., www.ForeignAffiairs.com. The full text is viewable at The Eleanor Roosevelt Papers Project, George Washington University, Dept. of History, http://www.gwu.edu/~erpapers/.

Selected Reading

My text does not pretend to original scholarship. I have gleaned my ideas primarily from the following works and sites and have relied on some more than others.

Thomas Jefferson

BOOKS

Becker, Carl. *The Declaration of Independence: A Study in the History of Political Ideas.* New York: Vintage Books, 1922.

Dumbauld, Edward, ed. *The Political Writings of Thomas Jefferson.* New York: Bobbs-Merrill, 1955.

Gordon-Reed, Annette. *Thomas Jefferson and Sally Hemings: An American Controversy.* Charlottesville: University Press of Virginia, 1997.

Hofstadter, Richard. *The American Political Tradition.* New York: Vintage Books, 1948.

Maier, Pauline. *American Scripture: Making the Declaration of Independence.* New York: Alfred A. Knopf, 1997.

Wills, Gary. *Inventing America: Jefferson's Declaration of Independence.* Garden City, New York: Doubleday, 1978.

ESSAYS/WEB

"An Expression of the American Mind: Understanding the Declaration of Independence." National Endowment for the Humanities, EDSITEment— History: http://edsitement.neh.gov/view_lesson_plan.asp?id=723

Gates, Henry Louis, Jr. "Mister Jefferson and the Trials of Phillis Wheatley." 2002 Jefferson Lecture in the Humanities, www.neh.gov/whoweare/gates/lecture.html

Jaffa, Harry V. "The American Founding as the Best Regime." 2007. The Claremont Institute, http://www.claremont.org/publications/pubid.682/pub_detail.asp

Malone, Dumas. "Thomas Jefferson," *Dictionary of American Biography.* New York: Charles Scribner's Sons, 1936.

Thomas Jefferson's Monticello. http://www.monticello.org/

Colonial Williamsburg. http://www.history.org/

Harriet Tubman

BOOKS

Clinton, Catherin. *Harriet Tubman: The Road to Freedom*. Boston: Little, Brown, 2004.

Lowry, Beverly. *Harriet Tubman: Imagining a Life*. New York: Anchor Books, 2007.

Ward, Andrew. *The Slaves' War: The Civil War in the Words of Former Slaves*. Boston: Houghton Mifflin, 2008.

WEB

Bradford, Sarah. *The Moses of Her People*. (1806), e-book #9999, Project Gutenberg, 2006, http://www.gutenberg.org/catalog/world/readfile?fk_files=30732&pageno=1

Harriet Tubman Home. http://www.harriethouse.org/

Abraham Lincoln

BOOKS

Donald, David Herbert. *Lincoln*. New York: Simon & Schuster, 1995.

Kaplan, Fred. *Lincoln: The Biography of a Writer*. New York: Harper, 2008.

Striner, Richard. *Father Abraham*. New York: Oxford University Press, 2006.

Williams, T. Harry, ed. *Abraham Lincoln: Selected Speeches, Messages, and Letters*. New York: Holt, Rinehart and Winston, 1957.

Wills, Garry. *Lincoln at Gettysburg*. New York: Touchstone, Simon & Schuster, 1992.

Wilson, Douglas, L. *Lincoln's Sword*. New York: Vintage Books, 2006.

ESSAYS/WEB

Abraham Lincoln Birthplace. National Historic Site. http://www.nps.gov/abli/

Abraham Lincoln Home. National Historic Site. http://www.nps.gov/liho/

Lehrman, Lewis. "Mr. Lincoln and the Founders." The Lincoln Institute, The Lehrman Institute, www.mrlincolnandthefounders.org

Scott v. Sanford, 60 U.S. 393 (1857). (The Dred Scott Case—see Justice Curtis' dissent) http://supreme.justia.com/us/60/393/case.html

Frederick Douglass

BOOKS

Douglass, Frederick. *Life and Times of Frederick Douglass* (revised edition, 1892). London: Collier Books, 1962.

Stauffer, John. *The Black Hearts of Men: Radical Abolitionists and the Transformation of Race.* Cambridge: Harvard University Press, 2002.

WEB

Frederick Douglass National Historic Site. http://www.nps.gov/archive/frdo/freddoug.html

Elizabeth Cady Stanton

BOOKS

Griffith, Elizabeth. *In Her Own Write: The Life of Elizabeth Cady Stanton.* New York: Oxford University Press, 1984.

ESSAYS

Stanton, Elizabeth Cady. "Introduction to the 'Women's Bible'." In *Women's Voices, Feminist Visions,* Third Edition, Shaw, Susan M., & Lee, Janet, eds. Boston: McGraw Hill, 2007.

Stanton, Elizabeth Cady. "The Solitude of Self." In *Images of Women in American Popular Culture,* Second Edition, Dorenkamp, McClymer, Moynhan, Vadum, eds. Fort Worth: Harcourt Brace, 1995.

WEB

Women's Rights National Historic Site. http://www.nps.gov/wori/historyculture/elizabeth-cady-stanton.htm

Henry David Thoreau

BOOKS

Krutch, Joseph Wood. *Henry David Thoreau.* New York: Dell Publishing Co., 1948.

Thoreau, Henry David. *Walden.* New York: New American Library, 1960.

ESSAYS/WEB

Thoreau, Henry, David. "On the Duty of Civil Disobedience." In *Walden and 'Civil Disobedience.'* New York: New American Library, 1960.

Thoreau, Henry, David. "Slavery in Massachusetts," "Life Without Principle," "A Plea for Captain John Brown." http://thoreau.eserver.org/default.html

Walden Pond State Reservation. http://www.mass.gov/dcr/parks/walden/

Ida B. Wells

BOOKS

Davis, Angela Y. *Women, Race & Class.* New York: Vintage Books, 1983.

Dubois, W. E. B. *The Souls of Black Folk.* In *Three Negro Classics*, New York: Avon Books, 1965.

Duster, Alfreda M., ed. *Crusade for Justice: The Autobiography of Ida B. Wells.* Chicago: The University of Chicago Press, 1970.

Franklin, John Hope. *Reconstruction after the Civil War.* Chicago: University of Chicago Press, 1994.

WEB

Ida B. Wells Website. http://www.idabwells.org/

Wells, Ida B. *A Red Record.* Chicago: Donohue and Henneberry, 1895, http://dig.lib .niu.edu/gildedage/idabwells/writings.html

W. E. B. Du Bois Institute. http://dubois.fas.harvard.edu/

Eleanor Roosevelt

BOOKS

Cook, Blanche Weisen. *Eleanor Roosevelt*, Volume 1. New York: Viking, 1992.

Cook, Blanche Weisen. *Eleanor Roosevelt*, Volume 2. New York: Viking, 1999.

Glendon, Mary Ann. *A World Made New: Eleanor Roosevelt and the Universal Declaration of Human Rights.* New York: Random House, 2001.

Lash, Joseph P. *Eleanor: The Years Alone.* New York: W. W. Norton & Co., 1972.

Roosevelt, Eleanor. *This I Remember.* New York: Harper & Brothers, 1949.

WEB

American Experience. PBS, Interview with Vernon Jarrett, http://www.pbs.org/ wgbh/amex/eleanor/filmmore/reference/interview/jarretto2.html

Eleanor Roosevelt National Historic Site. http://www.nps.gov/elro/

The Eleanor Roosevelt Papers Project. http://www.gwu.edu/~erpapers/

Task Force on Celebrating Eleanor Roosevelt and The Universal Declaration of Human Rights. http://www.erooseveltudhr.org/index.php?option=com_content &task=section&id=5&Itemid=27

About the Author

JOHN PERRAULT is a balladeer, poet, teacher, and attorney practicing in New Hampshire and Maine. He has authored two previous works: *The Ballad of Louis Wagner and other New England Stories in Verse* (Peter Randall Publisher, 2003) and a poetry collection: *Here Comes the Old Man Now* (Oyster River Press, 2005). A prolific songwriter, John has recorded seven albums of his songs over the years. He presents ballad programs in schools, libraries and museums for the New Hampshire Humanities Council. He is also a touring artist with the New Hampshire State Commission on the Arts and the New England Foundation for the Arts. John was Portsmouth Poet Laureate for 2003–2005. For further information and samples of his work, visit www.johnperrault.com.

About the CD

The musicians appearing on the attached CD are:

JOHN PERRAULT, *guitar & vocal on all cuts*

MIKE ROGERS, *harmonica on cuts 4, 6 and 8*

ELLIE MAY SHUFRO, *violin on cuts 1 and 3*

BARBARA LONDON, *keyboard & backup vocals on cuts 4 and 7;
flute on cut 7*

RICK KRESS, *drums on cuts 4 and 7*

JIM MACDOUGALL, *bass & backup vocal on cut 4*

DAVID SURETTE, *mandolin on cut 2; second guitar on cut 5*

SUSIE BURKE, *backup vocal on cuts 2 and 5*

RICK WATSON, *second guitar on cut 8*

❖ ❖ ❖

Recorded February, 2008 through January 2009 at
Landrock Studios, Rollinsford, New Hampshire

Engineer, mixing and mastering: Jeff Landrock

CD production: Tom Daly, Crooked Cove Records, Hampton, NH

All ballads are © 2009 John Perrault and published
by Rock Weed Music, ASCAP